# Blame it on Me

*Collins*

© Briony Collins, 2021

All rights reserved; no part of this book may be reproduced by any means without the publisher's permission.

ISBN: 978-1-913642-60-0

The author has asserted their right to be identified as the author of this Work in accordance with the Copyright, Designs and Patents Act 1988

Cover design by Aaron Kent

Edited & typeset by Aaron Kent

Broken Sleep Books (2021)

Broken Sleep Books Ltd
Rhydwen,
Talgarreg,
SA44 4HB
Wales

## *Contents*

| | |
|---|---|
| Harbour | 7 |
| Montbretias | 8 |
| Sunset | 9 |
| To Fall Towards Stars | 10 |
| What Goodbye Looks Like | 11 |
| A Conversation, c. 2001 | 12 |
| What Remains | 14 |
| Jasmine | 15 |
| Comet | 16 |
| Ampersand | 18 |
| Confession | 19 |
| No Such Thing | 21 |
| Skeleton | 23 |
| Stigmata | 24 |
| My Ugliest Thought | 26 |
| Opening Night | 27 |
| The Sound of Waking | 28 |
| Carrion | 29 |
| Four O'Clock | 30 |
| Andromeda | 31 |
| Grandma's Ring | 32 |
| Plateau | 33 |
| Salt | 34 |
| Curvature | 35 |
| Losing Time | 37 |
| Dead Badger | 38 |
| Childhood | 39 |
| Blame it on Me | 40 |
| Sleep | 41 |
| | |
| Acknowledgements | 43 |

# Blame it on Me

Briony Collins

## *Harbour*

I miss her smell – sand & tobacco,
wool & sea salt, sweetness of moss –
all the notes of my mother's body.

I miss her fingers – each shoreline
of her skin met with a crescent
bay of dirt she treasured there.

I miss her arms – a harbour opening,
a safe place for me to wreck myself
against the glaciers of growing up –

the way I craved them to hold me
on the morning she left herself,
no longer my marina,
but as blue as the sea.

## *Montbretias*

The most magnificent hair I will ever see
catches sunlight and gifts it back as copper,
Montbretias bloom against your skin,
roots that burgeon deeper than blood.

The worst part is knowing it no longer exists,
the soft decay of petals burrowing,
breaking against dark earth,
fungus grey and salt blue, a wildflower
cooling to dust.

## *Sunset*

All you ask for on your last Earth night is a glass of water.
I hope you know what it really means – life thirsts to fill you.

> *Stay with me. Please.*

How the skin cracks around your eyes, blackening with
the slow dilation of forever. How the milk of your bones

pours and empties, drowns you from the inside out.
How brittle you become in the pallid echoes of moonlight.

> *Don't go. Not just yet.*

There is so much of this world left to share together:
how we will go to Rome and stand at the feet of Gods,

Hadrian's Venus, Saturnalia until sunset, Jupiter burning.
The depth of history you will miss as you cascade into it.

How at Ostia Antica we dream of long-dead stars reviving in
the amphitheatre, chips of stonework, ovation of ghosts.

> *Applause and awake.*

All you ask for on your last Earth night is a glass of water.

## *To Fall Towards Stars*

All my life nightmares have plagued me,
riddled my insides with goosebumps,
sent me jolting, twitching back
into an awakening during all the
dead hours of night.

They were worse as a child,
but you knew that, gliding
into my bedroom to sit with me,
counting the valleys of my palms
until I slept again.

My first memory is of you, hair
wild and alight with the back-glow
of fluorescent bulbs, lifting me up
onto the draining board by
the kitchen sink,

so I could see out of the window,
tallying stars until I felt it:
the sensation of toppling back,
the heaviest thing in the world
becoming my eyelids.

Then nothing but the sound
of vertigo – the static of stars –
and me, thanks to you,
collapsing unafraid
upwards into the sky.

## *What Goodbye Looks Like*

Her favourite mug collecting dust,
feathers of skin & memories
cradled in cold curves of bone,
from where she once sipped & now
nothing but the absence of kisses.

Her husband's bed where he shapes
the duvet into her, all meaning
dries up in down. The stitches of grief
undo in his arms that still pulse
for her sunsets & tomorrows.

Her children in the morning, standing
on the rickety chair, pulling cereal boxes
from cupboards for breakfast, while
her husband soaks up his permanent
night, buries himself in her pillow.

But no longing so vicious as the first
day, when her children paced circles
in the living room, her son crying
because he didn't understand &
her daughter crying because she did.

# *A Conversation, c. 2001*

*You're still awake?*

Can't sleep.

*Me either. Here, budge up. Gimme some of the covers. There we go.*

Daddy, are you okay?

*Do you know what a spirit is?*

No.

*A spirit is a person's essence, made of all their love and hope. It lives inside them.*

Do I have one?

*Yes. Everyone does. Even people who've died.*

Like Mummy?

*Like Mummy. She left her spirit behind to watch over you and Cale.*

Left behind? Where did she go?

*Somewhere. Nowhere.*

Grandma says she's with God.

*No. He isn't real. There's only her spirit.*

That's like magic. Why is there magic but no God?

*Because if God was real she would be here
instead of me. But knowing her was magic.*

Her spirit will look after you too.

*…get some sleep.*

## *What Remains*

The candle sets her face in the photo frame
alive with movement, casts deep shadows
in her cheekbones and illuminates the glass
of her skin until she is almost real again,

                                        but she is nowhere.

Some nights you could believe in Heaven
if you let yourself, abandon your heart to stars,
lattice your fingers together and surrender
to a fifth season which comes after

the long year of life wavers and stumbles.
You could resign your days to knowing you will
see her when the whites of your eyes freeze,
set their sights on what is to come.

Some nights you could believe in Heaven,
watch the smoke as the wick burns out
cup her chin in the picture, her wry smile
flickering in the breath of the last ember.

## *Jasmine*

Rain. How she was Jasmine and I was Briony, both named for plants and thirsting for a downpour in the same way, our skin bruised from playing hide-and-seek between the old caravans, some attached to cars and others propped on piles of bricks – the perfect picture of mortality: my best friend and me, five years old and giggling, next to their splintered remains.

Rain. How we sang in it before we'd heard of Gene Kelly or Nick Lucas, who found whispers of themselves decades beyond their voices in the off-beat trills of children who knew the words but not the melody. Somehow we made our warbling work, spinning an umbrella each like showgirls, not knowing where we learned those moves, only that they were ours and we were theirs.

Rain. How our fathers rigged up the festival swing boats together and saved us the red one at the end – bare-breasted women painted on each side so the drops ran down them like sweat and we understood that our bodies would become like theirs one day, but not today. Today we were pirates and a gale swept us through the seas of our song, living our childhoods for the first time, for the only time.

## *Comet*

I'm the most delicate comet
to ever succumb to gravity.

I've been untethered
from my place in space,

watching the Earth breathe
underneath my body

as the floor rises –
dips its head in for a kiss.

The green carpet blurs,
softens in my aviation

so I can't see the stains
of food and wax and time.

The voile in the window
whispers in the vibrations

of the air, dances against
the lull of the city outside,

smiles yellow from smoke
of old cigarettes and grey

along the ends; feathers
of dusty osculation.

Blue walls spin across
the movement of vision,

remind me of the way
the sky looks on postcards.

I tell myself to smile –
it's only a game, only a game

my father plays. He doesn't
want to hurt me, even when

he sends me soaring
across the living room.

I'm a single, solitary rock
inbound for the sofa,

which catches me in its
cushions and cuddles me

close to stop me shaking.
I'm the most delicate comet,

still learning to live
with the trepidation

of elegant flight,
of poised fright,

curtain fall,
star fall,

the grace
of fear.

## *Ampersand*

Along the coast of Wales there's place I forgot about,
where I taught my brother how to draw ampersands
with an empty razor shell.

       *Like that?* he asked me &
I lied to him so I could see the sun shine out his eyes.
He threw down the shell in a little triumph

& cracked it in a footprint,
splintering its skeleton into a mosaic, embedding it in
the grains of every carapace. We chased oystercatchers

       who muddied their legs
against lugworm castings until his hand burrowed
into my fist & spread my fingers around his.

*I can see forever*, he told me,
& I wished we were limpets kissed to rocks & not crushed
in the tread of our shoes, but all the shells were broken in

       that last frontier of childhood.
We ignored the soap in the rock pools & the bags we
pretended were jellyfish & the bodies of drink cans

bleeding their rust by the
stone steps we used to sit on & imagine were a
castle wall from which we could protect this place,

       but we were only children
& we didn't belong there & we only wanted to play
& love before we forgot how to recognise our world.

## *Confession*

Forgive me, Father,
for the worst thing
I have ever done;
I used to tell people
you were dead.

When I was nine I
sunk my thumbs
into a garden snail,
skewered into the
soft body and pried
its shell off, cracking
away pieces like a
hard-boiled egg.

You peeled me,
dug your fingers
into my yolk until
I erupted, bled my
golden insides out
across your palms,
transmutation of
ovum and snails.

I was an orphan; a
homeless, quivering
slip of flesh, and you
were nothing but
the carapace of a man
who used to be loved,
mucus of sorrow
down your cheeks

and under your nails,
resigning all your days
to missing her,

to being the fragments
of my home, the
broken mollusc.
Now I commit myself
to splitting open,

knowing I can't
retract my words,
only add more words,
these words, my whole
life is a mess of words,
forgive me,
forgive me,
forgive me.

## *No Such Thing*

I hear stories about you
from the funeral:

how you tore a card
off a bouquet laid

over her grave
because someone

else said they loved
her, that maybe

you weren't her
always, her only.

How even in death
you couldn't let

her have these
final professions

that came too late
and too brief,

on a 5x3 note
taped to lilies

which were destined
to wilt on her bones,

huddle down over
her soil, seep into

her hollow smile.
How you knew

there was no such
thing as forever

but, just in case,
the world needed

to know that it
would be you.

## *Skeleton*

6,209 days. That's how long I lived with you:
like a colony inside a hive, all made of the same buzz
save the Queen – who gorges herself on the blood of her brood.
Like a crack in a plant pot where woodlice huddle
– armadillos cuddled into the decay of soil,
the blackness of flesh and fungus underneath the magnolia tree,
still small but lavishing the garden with pink suns.
Like the fish in the pond pecked to death by gulls'
orange beaks with red spots and garlands of entrails.
Like poisonous berries that delight the blackbird,
a tumour that grows and splits its cancer,
time beating through rims of my ears.
You loved me like skeletons love flesh
to hide the horror of a face with no eyes – the vision dead.

## Stigmata

Sometimes a father's wounds are left to scar his
children's bodies, how his pain can mar and mutilate even
when he doesn't mean to. In the house where she
died, hitting my head and splitting it open, you asleep on the
sofa that came second hand from the chip shop, a
breathy stupor in a garden of ash and empty bottles, a musk
of sweat permeating the hot air of the living room,
where the curtains haven't been opened in months, the days
mean nothing anymore. When I need you to be awake,
come back and fix it, stop the flesh tearing and deploying
armies in a downpour of venom – how is so much
blood inside me? The slick squeezing of a heart erupting,

having no choice but to leave you, make a dizzy
ascent to the bathroom and hold myself until it stops. I can't
wish for you then, only her, the softness of her
voice, the melody of her body thrumming like jazz.
 *Deadly, deadly,*
 *are you there?*
 *Drift up the dark to me.*
 And then I faint.

Scabbing, consciousness buzzing back, I wake on the floor,
 clean myself up, come downstairs to find you, my
vision receding to the sight of you still asleep, dreaming in
peace while my eyelashes mat with a mixture of blood made
 from you and the love you lost.

## *My Ugliest Thought*

My father told me how you died:
you were sick and the doctor
gave you the wrong medicine.

And then I got sick.

When I was seventeen my world
turned purple – the colour of skin
when death settles the blood.

My head filled with the crying
of bees, flesh suffocated my bones.
It was always night-time.

I stayed in bed for three months,
drifting in the cloudy place between
surrendering and fighting for life.

I needed medicine to numb myself
to the sounds of living and the bright
lights of a thousand days I didn't want.

A bottle of painkillers would let me go
gracefully and quietly into the dark,
tiptoeing back into your arms.

I didn't take them.

The weight of my ugliest thought
anchored my soul to my body:
was the medicine really wrong,

or did you purposely take too much
just to stop drifting and give up?

# *Opening Night*

> BIRDSONG
> Act II, scene v

*Stagehands cue up the next sound effect.*
*Ten seconds until birdsong descends from the speakers.*
*Jeanne is talking and I lose myself as I focus*
*on being Stephen. Skylarks divide and conquer*
*the reaches of my mind.*

**STEPHEN**: My men talk about skylarks. Even when we're
blowing each other to bits, the birds keep singing.

*Every noise from the audience is as distant*
*as the birds who crow over the bodies of soldiers –*
*my friends. People look on, not seeing me blowing*
*myself to bits for the sake of a script. The lines*
*alone mean nothing,*

*but they swell and ride the tides of grief*
*that my character can't contain: it was this day,*
*nineteen years ago, that my mother died.*
*I cry and everyone still believes I'm Stephen;*
*they only watch the show they pay for.*

**STEPHEN**: They don't care about us.

*When I say* Isabelle *and collapse perfectly,*
*my heart echoes another name:* Katrina. *My mother*
*comes through the dark to me. The blind*
*auditorium only see the rehearsed phantoms.*
*But I can see more.*

*After the show, I bow as Stephen, rising as*
*myself, dreaming of a life unlived, her spirit*
*tangled in words that don't belong to me. Cheers*
*herald in reality and I peer through my own skin*
*knowing I sold my sorrow to the song of skylarks.*

## *The Sound of Waking*

Mornings are supposed to be lively:
    coffee beans, chaffinches, streams of
laughter caught in wind chimes.
    When you live alone they are silent:
you hunt patterns in the uneven ceiling
    paint while the weight of your skin
squeezes you between unwashed sheets.
    You attach yourself to your bed like
biofilm, tongue running over teeth, hands
    twisting the duvet tighter, a pillow
nothing but a nest for sebum and saliva.
    A dead arm lolls beside the body.

Sounds begin to creep, mingle together
    with the tinnitus of loneliness,
the first signs that you are starting to wake.
    The jackdaws outside beg each other,
remind you to check your social media
    for the same noise – thousands of
people echoing their own names: *jack, jack,*
    *jack*, from behind a glass parting.
There must be one thing – *one thing* –
    to get up for today
        *(pick at that thought like a day-old scab,*
            *tender and ripe for another blood-letting).*

Who would notice if you stayed in bed
    and fantasised about dark passages,
the damp earth, eulogies?

## *Carrion*

*Nothing lasts forever,* but I don't mind that; everything
ends and I want things to end faster. I spend hundreds of hours
wishing away days, the bedroom clock pecks my brain like carrion,
vultures up through my ear canals: it's me, it's the roadkill woman
swarming her flies on the side of her mind, survived in pieces
by soil trailing through earthworms. I listen, the clock spans
its wings, circles above the headboard, clicking talons
and waiting to strike. Nothing lands on the hour.

I want things to end faster, even though *you don't know what
you've got until it's gone*, but I don't like living without knowing,
sometimes I don't like living at all.

## *Four O'Clock*

Always the worst time of day:
how my kitchen window looks clean
until this angle of sunlight
illuminates fingerprints from
old tenants, the jabbing
recriminations on the glass outside.
My view ruptures with canopies
of webs in the corner, where
a spider huddles with bundles
of sticky, eviscerated corpses.

How the last of the afternoon
pours into my flat further, catches
occasional crumbs on the linoleum.
I worry the ants will come, but
never sweep the morsels away – my
life is a mess to contain all messes –
let this dirt lie until I pad
through barefoot, feel pieces plaster
to my skin like scabs to be
peeled off and thrown out.

## *Andromeda*

I should be sitting in a garden:
Brimful of Asha tearing out the radio
cuts to news – a body floats downriver,
crystalline black country factories
mourn him together under their grey fleeces
until the deadout – the last bee shrinks
from finches and flora in a spring balm.

Instead, I'm in the back of an ambulance,
red and blue nebulae flaring circles around me,
tied up in a constellation of IV tubes –
this chained woman now a patchwork of
interstellar veins and skin – a sun
blazing behind my eye sockets to the cloudy
delirium of infection.

*You wouldn't have made it to morning.*

Days of retching air into a washing up bowl,
watching the back of my skull as my
eyes roll up into it, hours in the dark and
lengthening space between heartbeats, until
paramedics arrive, lift me into a wheelchair.
A body hurtles down Ffordd Penrhos – a figure
of stars desperate to crash and cling to Earth.

## *Grandma's Ring*

For years you struggle to pull your wedding ring off your finger.
The arthritis that settles and swells in your knuckles keeps it
bound as tightly to your skin as the vows you made.

Nothing happens when it falls off, dropping to the floor,
rolling like a coin and calming at the lip of the worn carpeting.
You're only reaching for your glass, tremors tracing the shape of

your hands, the aftershocks from the malignant
epicentre inside your lungs. It's the earthquake that sends us
reeling like your ring until all we can do is lie still,

accept the diagnosis and collapse into ourselves. Your smile
as you slip the ring back on can bring the sun out of the moon,
light fires at the bottom of the sea, call us back to a time before

this tectonic grief, but can't hide how much weight you
are losing, how the knots of your fingers are coming undone.

## *Plateau*

'Acceptance' is a misleading name for the final stage of grief;
it should be called 'The Plateau.' It draws itself in a sharp, linear
 parallel to everything you once loved.

Weeds burgeon between stone slabs where her footsteps
should be, cavalcades of children avoiding them like death,
 *(step on a crack, break your mother's back)*

and you find yourself searching for your lost one
in the strangest place – the back of the closet with her old clothes:
 crawl inside and close the doors, huddle her dresses just to

feel something she touched. Decades on, circle in songs
that resurrect the sound of her laughter, that chime,
 *(come up and see me, make me smile)*.

The Plateau goes on: how almost twenty years pass and
you still fracture into pieces in the pub on her birthday – step
 outside – light a cigarette just to smell like her.

Kicking the base of a lamppost the thought still clings:
acceptance is a lie to pull you through the first days,
 before the open plains of    forever.

## *Salt*

It's snowing today, but I think it's worse
in the clouds where you are, dense

as they gather their duvets around each
other, blanket in from a February the

colour of salt. There was a woman in the
Bible who turned into a pillar of the stuff

for looking back; I almost lost my
humanity this morning for glancing over

my shoulder at the undisturbed grit
along the pavement outside my house –

no footprints, even though you come here
most nights when everyone is sleeping

and my bottle of wine is down to a burgundy
ring on the table.

## *Curvature*

Sometimes I stand in the
        sea, stare at the horizon,
                and imagine you are
        across the water, looking
back. If it weren't for the
        Earth's curvature, maybe
                our eyes would meet as we
        scanned the skyline, maybe
we could be together.

                *What is it like where you are?*

The remains of a crab wash
        up on the shore, pecked open
                by gulls; its back blood-eagled,
        pincers splayed out in surrender,
the scent of the deepest
        ocean trench echoing inside
                its exoskeleton. Do things die
        on your beach too? Would this
creature have survived there?
        Barnacles dry up by the rock
                pools, sinking into themselves
        until the tide comes, brings
them back for a time, owing
        everything to the moon's revival.
                Periwinkles scatter like broken
        bitumen, each one turning to
face the horizon with me.

Sometimes, I stand in the
        sea, not sure if I should
                start walking towards you,
        cross this barrier to find
you smiling on the other side.
        As my feet slip into the

                        sand, an epiphany strikes:
            if it weren't for the Earth,
I could see you.

## *Losing Time*

When we get the sky back,
we'll share kisses with the
same end of a cigarette, we'll
tear out all the flowers in your
garden and turn them into
crowns, we'll shelter underneath
scaffolding and peel off paint
from the derelict bookshop,
we'll sit in the pub until they
kick us out and pretend we
like the taste of vodka, we'll
write everything we can about
the pandemic until we're sure
it was fiction this whole time,
because no one will ever
believe the Earth is really
this dangerous, no, we'll go
back to rolling our eyes at
the news and basting our
wallets with the fat of the poor;
if it doesn't matter now, it never
mattered at all. We'll only know
one thing: nothing, *nothing*,
was so cruel as being apart
from each other,
from friends.

## *Dead Badger*

Our cousinhood can be pared down to a precious morning in July '06, sitting on a bunk in a cabin of a blue canal boat called *Frisbee*. You were barely two, your knowledge of language a reduction of milk and motherhood, of rhyme and rheum.

On paper, your mind unfurled in the wild etchings of a child with stories to tell but no words, until you pressed your palms to the window so hard they turned flat and white, smiled at a passing boat and proclaimed a single, triumphant syllable: *bot.*

A dead badger bobbed by us in the water, its fur muddied to conceal the white stripes of its face among the black ones. *Bot*, you said again, as solemn and still as the canal, and I knew you were really asking if I saw it too.

This is all language is – touching other people's worlds with our visions, hoping that someone knows what you mean and understands. But you taught me that poetry is everything else: the words we never learn and the ones left unsaid.

## *Childhood*

Out by the lake, we played marbles on the concrete.
My palms spread wide on the ground as we crouched
and grains of stone needled their way into my skin,
left dents in my fingers where they should be whole.
My brother sang under his breath to the last song
that came through the radio in our dad's truck,
snapped his best marble forward and smiled at the *clack*
of glass on glass, excitement exhaled through his teeth.

I missed, mine rolling away and dropping off the short lip
of the concrete into the grass, each blade peeling back.
I tried to chase it but it disappeared through my hands,
drowning invisible to the brown earth of the lake bed.

## *Blame it on Me*

**i.**
Staple me to the wall by my neck and spit in my eyes:
the wetness of anger as you scream to fill my brain with your voice.
I count your blood vessels, bursting in a dot-to-dot and the numbers
all add up to your face – at once my father and a drowning man
sinking into a sea of anguish, abandoning himself.
You grip tighter to pull me down too; even on these shores
you're scared to be alone. Fill my lungs with grief –
blue bile and gasoline, the watermark of a broken creature.
When you remember yourself, you pull me to your chest
and say *I love you, you know*, as I slip away into a sepia-toned
memory, fraying around its edges, of standing on your feet
as you moved so we danced together, my arms raised to hold
onto yours – a puppet surrendering to your footsteps.

**ii.**
You've forgotten what love looks like; everything you know
about loving a person inured to emptiness and being incomplete.
This is your love: chrysostomic ballads into the open lips of bottles,
dozens of cigarette packs as though they contain a free toy like
a cereal box or kid's magazine, your diurnal insides begging
for more light than the moon or your computer screen,
the only panacea is the endless search for the saddest song
you will play to death – 'Sugar Mice' is imprinted on your
soul now, its notes are your fingerprints, every chord an addition
to your secret Silmarillion: the mythos of a man who dreams
of any reality other than the one he inhabits.

**iii.**
Staple me to the wall by my neck and spit in my eyes:
the horror of yourself as deep as skin, but the real you is rooted
in marrow. You were a poet before you became my father and
breathed your visions into me – these words belong to you too.
I believe you loved me, but your heart suffocated, took its last
breath as your wife did, turned to marble to match her skin,
a memento of a man who once gave himself boldly, bravely,
never expecting the betrayal of mortality to come so soon.

## *Sleep*

She cries her whalesong
in the sea behind my eyes:

her hair echoing rubies
in the tissues of rippling sleep,

where she whispers seaweed,
freckles dreams in Greek fire,

and sinks while I wait
for her to wake once more.

## *Acknowledgements*

'Harbour,' 'Montbretias,' and 'Sunset' appeared in Black Bough Poetry's anthology, *Deep Time Volume II* (2020). 'Curvature' appeared in Folklore Publishing's anthology, *Secret Chords* (2021). 'Childhood' appeared in Poetry Wales's special issue, *Stay-at-Home* (2020).

'Opening Night' contains lines from the play *Birdsong*, adapted for stage by Rachel Wagstaff. 'Plateau' contains a lyric from Steve Harley and Cockney Rebel's song, 'Make Me Smile (Come Up and See Me).' 'Blame it on Me' is a lyric from Marillion's song, 'Sugar Mice.'

I owe a tremendous debt of gratitude to Zoë Skoulding. *Blame it on Me* began as my BA dissertation and without her supervision and guidance, this book might not exist. Equally to Aaron Kent who brought this book into the world. Finally, I must thank my family – Grandma, Taid, Tanya, Gary, Finley, Cale, and Foxx – for their unconditional support.

I wanted to write about my mum for a long time, but didn't have the words to capture what losing her was really like. One day, I realised I never would. That was the difficultly with *Blame it on Me*; it wasn't going to be enough. All the languages and art in the world can't even begin to cover what it's like to grieve. This is only an attempt, a daughter trying her hardest to resurrect her mum with words. It doesn't matter that I can't. When you are destined to lose a battle, all that matters is that you fight anyway, that you champion your beliefs until the end. That is what love means.

*Blame it on Me* is dedicated to my mothers, Katrina and Jenny. In 'The Sound of Waking,' I talk about searching for a reason to go on living. That reason is you.

# LAY OUT YOUR UNREST

www.ingramcontent.com/pod-product-compliance
Lightning Source LLC
Chambersburg PA
CBHW061346040426
42444CB00011B/3119